THE WRITE LIFE DIARY

Write Your Life from Good to Great

Kristiina Hiukka

The Write Life Diary™
Write Your Life from Good to Great

Published through Lulu Enterprises, Inc.
All rights reserved
Copyright © 2010 by Kristiina Hiukka
Cover Design, Kristiina Hiukka
Cover Art, Steve Babb
Author Photo, Tammy Hunter
Interior Book Design and Layout, www.integrativeink.com.

ISBN 978-0-615-39243-1

CONTENTS

ACKNOWLEDGMENTS

This book would have been forgotten on an old diskette without Lisa Among reminding me that I had a book in me, and without encouragement from Bob Wartinger who believed people deserved to read it. Without my friend Judith Dern's masterful wordsmithing I would be still writing just diaries, not books.

My thanks to each of you for your encouragement – you helped me write my life from good to great.

INTRODUCTION TO THE WRITE LIFE DIARY

The *Write Life Diary*™ is a writing process designed to compose positive solutions and scenarios within the privacy of a diary with the goal of identifying and actualizing positive experiences in one's life. This method takes diary writing beyond a passive recording of daily events. It combines the playful qualities of journal writing with creative problem-solving.

The Write Life Diary was born out of my need to find a more productive use for my daily diary writing habit, something I started at age nine growing up in Finland. While reading through my personal diaries of the past years I felt I was not really making headway towards the direction I wanted to go. Although my environment and situations changed, a lot of my writing was still reporting the same kinds of issues I had tackled earlier in my life. There were recurring patterns, reoccurring challenges. I wanted to change these and become more active in determining what was taking place, to build on what I already knew, and become my own coach directing my path. I used writing for this purpose.

To extend my writing beyond just passively recording what had happened in my life, I wanted to be more proactive in deciding what I wanted to experience in my life. Through writing and reading, I realized there was a process I was using for visualizing and writing about my future, for bringing positive experiences into actuality.

A major change in my life enabled me to start working on my writing process more seriously than ever before. I had given up my professional work, and moved to a foreign country when my husband was relocated for his job. In this new foreign world, I had new priorities, new worries, new needs, and a new focus. I wrote about all these things, in order to have a sense of more control of my life. Then I tried my writing method, first with small things such as helping me build my courage and skill for driving and getting a driver's license, and finally, for moving on to bigger desires, such as finding the house of my dreams. Delighted with the results, which proved successful and fulfilling, I decided to catalog and share the process. My efforts are before you in this book, inspired by my personal experience as a writer of both conventional and *The Write Life* diaries.

When I began my writing experiment I had no previous knowledge that other people found diary writing to be such a powerful tool to change their lives. It was only much later when, to my surprise, I realized that books had been written about diary writing. However, none of them had developed exactly the same process that I had created for myself and outline here.

The Write Life Diary is based on two powerful principles that can be exercised through the writing process: 1) Life changing benefits and techniques of journaling find proactive expression in this process, and 2) the creative power of positive thinking and the law of attraction are also activated. The process also draws from the body of knowledge in the areas of strategic planning, creative problem solving, and creative writing techniques.

While *The Write Life Diary* preserves the freedom of self-expression held in a conventional private diary, it goes further by introducing an innovative interactive structure that is especially suitable for visualizing and enhancing positive change. *The Write Life Diary* process will encourage you to compose positive solutions and scenarios within the trusted strucure of a personal diary. As examples, throughout the book, I have included brief samples from my own diaries to offer anecdotal references and illustrations. My guideline was: "When your heart speaks, take good notes."

The Write Life Diary offers a new and simple application of a common practice. It will empower you to become the star of your own life story. *The Write Life Diary* provides tangible evidence that you can change your life by writing a new storyline. A written wish becomes a seed that you sow in the soil of possibilities through the act of writing. When the seed is in the ground, it is easier to concentrate on nurturing it and helping it to grow to full bloom.

As you work your way through these pages, I encourage you to discover *The Write Life Diary* as a guidebook for writing the success stories of your own life. Acknowledge your accomplishments and challenges, and envision in writing what you want to create for your future. By using writing as a tool to re-frame your challenges of today or the past into the best solutions for tomorrow, you empower yourself to take charge of your life. Since this book enables you to keep records not only of your dreams and desires, but also of your achievements and accomplishments, it will become a valuable guide for personal celebration.

Be aware, however, that *The Write Life Diary* methodology is not a magic wand. Neither is it an academic exercise about debating the issue of writing, nor a study of composing future scenarios. It is not a book about "How to Become a Writer," nor does it offer tips for composing a best-selling novel. It does not chronicle the history of diary writing. Finally, this book is not a career development guidebook. However, it can become an excellent personal aid for this purpose.

Although the writing methodology outlined in *The Write Life Diary* is based on the principle that there is value in telling every individual's story, it is not a guidebook about writing an autobiography. While a diary can reveal to the writer / reader more about themself than they might be willing to admit in a face to face conversation. Although writing can be therapeutic and can be applied as a tool in a healing process or as a part of a therapy - in fact, many therapeutic practices use the activity of keeping of private records of changing moods, actions, cravings and feelings as part of the healing process - the process outlined here is not intended to be therapy and has not been written according to any particular paradigm or school of thought.

Taking a step farther away from therapeutic use *The Write Life Diary* writing system, unlike more common documenting of the past, puts the emphasis on the future. Rather than recording what happened as if you were a passive victim of whatever life threw at you, *The Write Life Diary* guides you into creating more fulfilling solutions for the future. This empowering use of diary writing increases your ability to take full responsibility for your life.

WRITING YOUR FUTURE

Y ou don't have to be a psychic to know your future. You are creating it right here and now — with your current beliefs, attitudes, thoughts, hopes and fears. The choices you make today are the building blocks of your future. Many of us who write diaries find it easy to agree with Tristine Rainer (The New Diary, 1978) who writes, *"As I create my diary, I create myself."* This exciting creation happens every day.

Who is the person you are creating with your story? What are you here to do and be and contribute? This is the fundamental question we confront throughout our lives. It is a question about our purpose in life. Without your answer to this question, you are never satisfied with whatever you might gain or earn. Knowing your purpose gives direction, a sense of trust and fulfillment. Writing a diary can be a helpful process in developing an answer to this question. For me, it is easier to approach such a significant question from another angle, one that reveals my motivations for what I want to be and to create. Simply: to live the best possible life for me, I first need to know what I want.

I often hear people say they are apprehensive about writing a diary because their lives are so ordinary their diaries would make boring reading. True, recordings of everyday events, like in many blogs, can be boring reading. However, I believe that even occasional focusing on simple drafting of your life will make living your life more interesting. You are not writing a diary in order to become a novelist. In the *Write Life Diaries*, you are writing about your life in order to keep track of what is going on, how you change, and how the focus and the priorities in of your life change. The simplest things in life make revealing reading – later.

When I get together with my dear friend, Paula, and we have brought each other up to date by exchanging news about our current activities, she says: "OK, that's *what* you've *done*, now, let's hear *how* you *are!*" This remark has helped me shift the focus in my dairy writing from listing things happening in my life to how I feel about them. It became important to describe what is going on in my mind, in my heart, and to outline how I am.

Defining myself through what I had achieved, the things I had purchased, people I had met, is only superficial if it's not also anchored to how I feel about these events and interactions. What impact did something or someone have on me, why did it make me think or feel differently? For me, as for many of my high-achieving, career-oriented friends, it is often hard to imagine that there is value in simply *being*. I do not need to earn my value by what I do, or assert my place in the world by describing my doings; it is enough that I am. This revelation, the letting go of doing, has been one of the toughest for me to understand. Sometimes, when people ask me what I do, I toy with an idea of saying, "I am." It should be enough. However, when I quit my work to move to another country and didn't have my title and a business card anymore, I felt lost in the "Nobody Land". In our society we are almost exclusively defined by our work and position in our respective companies and organizations. Without these life markers or goal posts, I have found, we easily lose our identity. The challenge then becomes to learn how to validate ourselves for simply "being." And truly, this can be very liberating!

As I mentioned earlier, ever since I was nine, I have written a diary. After years of writing about simple stuff of my life, I began to question whether all the record-keeping was worthwhile. Many times I found I was encountering and repeating the same kinds of challenges in my life but in new situations. Even the solutions sounded familiar. So, obviously I wasn't learning from these patterns. Eventually, I began to suspect that whatever I wrote about myself, actually affirmed it. If I complained and moaned, my life would be full of exactly that: complaints and moans. If I only concentrated on my fears and failures, I would continue experiencing them. Startled by this thought, one day I realized the same must be true for positive thoughts! If I decided to write about the existing joys and happinesses in my life, logically it should follow that more joy and happiness should emerge in my life. In Sanaya Roman and Duane Packer's Opening to Channel (1987), I found a profound statement that seemed to confrm my idea: *"Every single statement you make about yourself, to a friend or yourself, becomes a truth. If you want a better future, speak of it, picture it, say it to others."*

I then understood that I could do whatever I wanted with my life. I could even lie about it – if I wanted to! I could turn my life into fantasy and write fiction. I'm the boss of my life! The same way, I can also decide there are only good things in my life and fill my diary full of stories about how well things are going for me and

7

how successful I am. It is *my* life and it is *my* private diary. I can create whatever I want with it!

Daydreaming provides us with a skill to help us define what we want. When we dare to be specific and describe those dreams in detail, they can serve as catalysts for choices and actions. Often, however, instead of defining what we really want based on our dreams, we find it easier to determine what we do *not* want. I believe it does matter *how* and what I communicate, even when I am communicating to myself. You can choose to define your life using either negations or affirmations. In my experience, negative expressions can add limitations and denial to my life, while positive wording can enhance my general well-being. Therefore, take notice and keeping track of your dreams as a gateway to gratitude rather than as a swamp of lack or loss. You will discover the pleasure and fun of writing about how you feel when you have achieved your dreams in the Future column of your diary. This will in turn enhance your ability to live from a place of abundance.

Diary writing has provided me with an opportunity to consciously define and pursue my future; I no longer want the future to "just happen." This doesn't mean that there are no adventures and no surprises in my life. I would never have the time and resources to write a script for every minute, every issue of my life. However, by following *The Write Life Diary* process, I can encourage and inspire some of the good things I want to experience to actually happen in my life. The thought process and action of putting my dreams into words and writing them down on paper helps me clarify what I want in life. There is room for flexibility as well. I have accepted the fact that my goals can evolve and change, which means I am not compelled to seek what I might have once written about in my diary as a steadfast goal or desire.

When I began writing, using the process I now call *The Write Life Diary*, I started with simple things I wanted to create in my life. For instance, several years ago I wanted several definite, concrete changes in my life. One of them was to learn to drive more confidently. For years I was scared stiff of driving and avoided it as much as possible. But when I moved to the United States, a country where the car is an imperative for survival, I had to buy a car and start driving. So, to encourage myself, I began writing about how good and relaxed I was as a driver. Every day, I read diary entries praising and describing how well I drove to the store, or to meet friends for coffee. I felt my confidence develop and I became more assured as I turned the ignition key and headed down the road. What joy I experienced when I passed the driving test, got my Washington state driver's license, and eventually began to truly *enjoy* driving! Being able to converse with my passengers and listen to music while driving were major achievements for me.

You can use diary writing in this way to spur on your achievements and to create meaningful experiences. Even if you do not yet know what you want out of your life, wouldn't this be a good time to give it some thought? To get started you do not need to have all the answers and a crystal-clear picture of your life goals. These will evolve as you do and they will materialize as you explore them through the diary writing process.

Experiment with writing to try on different ideas of what would fulfill you, to capture your dreams, and to define your goals. Nurture and develop all your ideas by writing them down daily. Be as brave and bold as you can be. Think big, write big, and have fun dreaming and writing. Always allow for change and development. Nothing you dream or write down is carved in stone – only written on paper!

WHY THE WRITE LIFE DIARY?

Over the years, diary writing or journaling has been appreciated for its benefits in various fields; for example, in therapy, autobiographical writing, business management or self development. Diary writing has been credited for its potential to manage change and accelerate learning. It is a tool for tapping into the writer's inner wisdom.

As part of growing-up, we all reach a point where perpetual "taking in" of learnings and education changes to "bringing out" distinct individual applications of this knowledge. Many times, *we know more than we know we know*. Through the writing process outlined in this book, I will show you how you can tap into your inner resources. You need not only look *up to* others but also *into* yourself. Diary writing is an excellent tool for this purpose.

"[The New Diary] can help you understand your past, discover joy in the present, and create your own future," Tristine Rainer writes in her book *The New Diary* (1978). She continues: *"Diary writing is free of ... rules. Everything and anything goes. You cannot do it wrong. There are no mistakes. At any time you can change your point of view, your style, your book, the pen you write with, the*

direction you write on the pages, the language in which you write, the subjects you include, or the audience you write to. You can misspell, write ungrammatically, enter incorrect dates, exaggerate, curse, pray, brag, write poetically, eloquently, angrily, lovingly.... It's your book, yours alone... Flow, spontaneity and intuition are the key words."

The Write Life Diary will guide you into your personal process of self discovery. Anyone can learn and follow this process. It takes no training or special skill. For example, this will be a useful process if you want to but find it difficult to meditate. Writing is an equally effective way to center the mind, also offering clarity and focus. As an activity, writing becomes a tool for focusing and for making thinking more tangible and concentration easier. The writing process itself becomes a form of meditation and affirmation.

It is well known that people have different learning styles. While some prefer to primarily apply their visual (seeing) sense to the learning process, others prefer a more kinesthetic (touch) or an auditive (hearing) approach. Although most of us are a mix of all these learning styles, typically we have a distinct preference for one. Diary writing will particularly help anyone who prefers a more tactile approach (the act of writing), or anyone who wants to use writing as a stimulus for this or her personal visualization exercises. *"Who knows more about you than you do?"* asks Joyce Chapman in her book *Journaling for Joy* (1991), where she also says, *"Somewhere inside of you is the answer to any question you could ever ask."*

THE BENEFITS OF WRITING THE WRITE LIFE DIARY

I t is an empowering experience to write one's own life story. Expressing ideas and desires, dreams and hopes in writing can inspire their actuality. *The Write Life Diary* will become your guide to mastering expressions of yourself and enable you to be in charge of your own realities. Along with this exciting potential, other benefits to becoming an open-minded diary writer can include:

- Focusing on the positive changes in your life

- Developing a vision about individual, relationship, family, work group, team, or organizational levels

- Creating a simple structure to explore your creativity

- Developing a tool for self-development

- Providing consistent self-coaching

- Bouncing off ideas on yourself

- Testing out various future solutions and scenarios

- Providing guidance and giving direction

- Identifing needs and obstacles

- Providing a problem-solving device

- Helping to enhance personal writing skills and self-expression

- Helping to understand motivations and motives

- Enabling you to take the full responsibility for your future

- Creating a more fufilling life

- Clarifying personal goals

- Demonstrating the true value of your life

- Revealing how exciting life can be

- Revealing new characteristics of your personality

- Serving as a source of support

- Serving as a constructive way to understand others

- Serving as a therapeutic tool

- Offering energizing and empowering effects

- Increasing self-awareness and build confidence

- Teaching how to learn and to trust your intuition

- Heightening sensitivity to people and the world around you

- Serving as a source of fun!

The Write Life Diary is based on the assumption that whatever you fill your mind with will manifest itself in some form in your reality.

13

Writing extensively about issues you feel good about or want to change encourages you think about them. This, in turn, gently assists you to make choices in your daily life to create and open yourself to unexpected possibilities for these good things to manifest themselves and become true.

WRITING AS A PERSONAL DEVELOPMENT TOOL

The What and Why of a diary can be approached from many different angles. As a testament to this versatility, it has been applied in many fields of life; for example, in various therapies, in autobiographical writing, in politics, in business management and in personal self-development. Old and young have written diaries in many cultures and languages. Diary writing has been credited for its potential for managing change and accelerating learning. It is a powerful tool, tapping the writer's inner wisdom, and, as I believe, helping to clear out the clutter in our minds.

There is an abundance of books about meditation and visualizing. Many of these encourage readers to write personal affirmations or desires to center their meditation or visualization practices. In other ways, writing can be used for creating good health and wealth and all kinds of self improvement. Unlike many books on the subject, *The Write Life Diary*, presumes that writing is a meditative process in its own right.

The author of *The New Diary* (1978), Tristine Rainer writes: *"This widespread use of the diary as a tool for personal growth and for realizing creative potential is a phenomenon of the twentieth century."* In the book's preface, Anais Nin, who taught diary writing with Rainer, says, *"We taught the diary as an exercise in creative will; as an exercise in synthesis; as a means to create a world according to our wishes, not those of others; as a means of creating the self... as a way of reintegrating ourselves when experience shatters us."*

For those who are in a transitional place in their lives or in-between jobs *The Write Life Diary* is an additional, perhaps more exploratory and non-regimented, writing form than the more structured career planning practices. While recognizing the benefits of more analytical approach, the *Write Life Diary* tries to keep you searching and expressing your purpose freely and in your authentic voice.

In order to prepare for and create the best possible future for yourself, being aware of the present is critical. You must know what and who you are dealing with today in the here and now because these interactions have the power to change you tomorrow. Everything I do, and everyone I meet today, affects what and how I will perform in the future. I use my diary as a simple way to gain insights into these possibilities. Thinking about every event as a learning opportunity makes life thrillingly exciting. I can't wait to see where this story is taking me!

As part of the process, it is important you learn to name everything you experience in order to re-create yourself daily. We humans are meaning-making machines. Unless you do it consciously, it will happen to you unconsciously and become a source for your assumptions and expectations. Once you understand that everything you experience shapes your life, writing a diary becomes a handy tool for dealing with these affects. Diaries have long served people by helping them keep records, observe life around them, and pour out their heart's problems and joys. Many writers have kept a diary to escape, or used it as a sanctuary, a private chamber. Some have written with the goal of publishing their memoirs, some want future generations to find their writings at a later time to gain a better understanding of events and, perhaps, earn forgiveness. Some writers simply write to learn about themselves. Many books and movies are based on discovered diaries. A Russian student of mine, Vladimir, also reminded me diaries can also be dangerous, politically or otherwise.

As examples of the various ways diary writing is used, there is the famous diary written by Anne Frank, a German-Jewish girl trapped in Amsterdam, Holland, during WWII. Anne wrote eloquently from her attic hiding place about her teen-age life under Nazi rule in words and observations that haunt us still today. Nicole Brown Simpson, who was murdered after she escaped from an infamously stormy marriage with O.J. Simpson, kept a written record of her abuse. Anaïs Nin has probably written the world's most famous diaries depicting her life with lovers such as Henry Miller. Many diarists, most notably, retired politicians, have tapped their vintage diary material to write their memoirs.

Sometimes diaries can reveal disturbing truths about their writer's mental state. Recently in *O Magazine,* the mother of the 17-year-old student who with his friend masterminded the massacre at their high school in Columbine, Colorado, agonized over the writings of the depressed and suicidal teen.

A while ago, I read about an urban tragedy that took place in

Tokyo. The story, partly published in a Japanese newspaper, unfolded in the diary of a 77-year-old woman. It described how she and her bedridden son starved to death in the heart of the affluent city. On a happier note, there have been examples of people locating family or discovering the life stories of friends and acquaintances because of diary episodes being published on the Internet. Anne Singer's search for the writer of a diary she had purchased at a flea market for 80 cents developed into an research project, a project she named "Emily." Finally, Emily was identified, but unfortunately, she had died the year before the mystery was solved.

Diary writing possesses singular honesty and authenticity because the process is protected from outsiders. It's private, and is thus free from all criticism. It becomes a sanctuary for our communication with ourselves. It contains our reflections on the past, descriptions of present events and relationships, and hopes for the future. Writing about our private self is an emotionally intense activity. Diary writing enables the writer to be uninhibited, to tap their inner resources, and to develop self awareness.

THE POWER OF POSITIVE WRITING

The foundation of this book lies in the belief that we all have the power to attract good things into our lives by thinking good things, by speaking good things, and by writing about good things, according to the principle of "like attracts like" or the Law of Attraction. By practicing the exercises outlined in *The Write Life Diary*, you will become more sensitive and more aware because you listen to your intuition, and act according to your inner guidance. Once you become more centered through the effort of writing, your creative mind begins to feed in more images and help your visualization become more specific. It is a virtuous cycle.

Many authors of "the positive thinking genre" urge their readers to practice various writing exercises in order to clear their minds for a more constructive view of life. For example, in his classic book Lou Tice (*A Better World, A Better You,* 1989) introduces a specific recipe for effective affirmations that he calls positive self-talk sentences. In his exercises, writing is used to connect the inner self to positive universal energy. The more often positive images and thinking are repeated, the more it enhances the chances of making them happen. I believe writing a positive diary about your future is excellent training for positive conversations with yourself.

I also believe what is on the outside reflects what we hold inside. If I am well, happy and satisfied, people around me are, too. I have found there a curious dialogue that occurs between two forces: negativity attracts the negative, positivity the positive. To break out of the vicious cycle of self-pity and negative thoughts into the virtuous cycle of self-esteem and life management, you must take full responsibility for your life.

POWER OF THE WRITTEN WORD

I n Western culture, writing has clout. Spoken word is often considered unreliable, suited only for storytelling. In order to build trust, important business is put into written form: contracts, strategic plans, reports, memos, letters, applications, manuals and instructions. The one who can word smith documents is in the position of power and influence.

In the world-famous Synectics© creative problem-solving method developed in 1950s by George Prince and Bill Gordon, note-keeping is done on a flip-board in front of the group where all participants can see the notes at all times. Everyone's contribution is meticulously recorded for further development; no idea gets lost once it is documented. This is an essential part of discovering innovations and solutions.

Based on our cultural conditioning for taking the written word so seriously, we can "fool" our unconsciousness with what we write. The more positive energy we put into the writing process the more powerful it becomes. In *Stepping Into the Magic* (1993), Gill Edwards writes:

"Our thoughts and beliefs create our reality. Our thoughts are energy, and that energy attracts people, events and opportunities which 'match' that energy, which resonate with it. Every thought is a prayer.

Whatever we believe or desire or fear or expect, we magnetize towards us.

Everyone is the scriptwriter, producer, director and star of their own play."

There are many metaphors for how someone can describe the story of their life. Just as you can choose to picture your life as a movie, I believe we might also see ourselves as managers of the business of our lives. As part of running a successful business, the manager has to take time for solid planning to secure future company profitability. Business plan writing has become important for every size organizations. Whether used for applying financing or for long-term planning, business plan writing is an essential part of every business manager's reality.

In order to prosper, we also need planning in our lives. Often planning is compared to a road map. It is easier to find the way to your destination when you know the directions and can plan the best route, know where the curves are and the steepest hills. In the same way, vague wishes and hazy hopes always become clearer and more tangible when written down. Bottom line, writing is a powerful way to design a life with intention.

START YOUR WRITE LIFE DIARY

I ask my students to get in the habit of writing every day. Even the busiest person can find a few minutes every day to at least jot down the date. Just dating the pages creates a relationship with the diary. Touching base and checking in with your diary is important. However, this process need not be something extraordinary, but rather a very ordinary part of one's life. It should be simple and easy to do. However, I also believe that the empty page should be respected. Empty pages can tell much more than we imagine: "I was busy that day," or "I led a very active and fulfilling life during the period when I didn't write." Sometimes dating a page serves as hook. The act captures you, encouraging you to outline your day by thinking, "Why don't I write just a few sentences, I've got a minute to spare?" And you are off! Another entry has made its way into the diary.

When you purchase a notebook or a sketchbook make sure it's wide enough to include the two columns. You can also use opposing pages as the columns for the Future and for the Present. You can also use the companion journal *The Write Life Diary* that is specifically designed for this purpose and is available at www.thewritelifediary.com. The benefit of writing long hand is that you can have your diary bedside or wherever and write whenever without a needing to worry about electric outlets or the battery on your computer. A tangible, notebook style diary also allows you to make it into "craft project" for visualization if you glue images from magazines or your movie tickets or other imagery triggering material onto its pages.

> *"The act of writing makes thoughts become real and brings a deeper level of release than just verbal communication or thinking can do alone."*
>
> *"In becoming a more confident writer, I was becoming a confident creator of my life. I began to ask myself questions and discover my own answers."*
>
> — Joyce Chapman, *Journaling for Joy, 1991*

To get started, write a page or two about your day today, this very day. Here are some steps and questions to prompt writing your first diary entry.

Writing your diary with intention

Close your eyes. Return to the time when you woke up this morning. How did you feel? What did you think of or worry about? Or what did you celebrate and were happy about? Who did you talk to first? What challenges did you need to overcome today? What made you happy? How do you feel right now?

When you feel ready, open your eyes and write briefly about your day, your thoughts, your feelings and activities. Remember your audience is *you* – or your Diary if you have chosen to give it a persona. Allow your inner voice of experience to speak as honestly as it can. Draw pictures or doodles if this helps get you started.

Now, read what you wrote. What are you learning about yourself? Is there a pattern or a theme emerging? What title would you give to your day? Write it on the top of the page as a heading. Date the page.

In Appendix 1, you will find a collection of more than one hundred tips to make writing a daily diary entry enjoyable and stimulating. Some ideas were adapted from *Journal to Self* (1990) by Kathleen Adams, and several are contributions from students in my classes for the Eastside Literacy Council in Bellevue, Washington. What is YOUR favorite way to be inspired to write? Sometimes it's best just to sit down and start writing without waiting for an inspiration. The more regular the habit, the better you become at it!

Many of my students use English as their second (or third or fourth or fifth or...) language. In your diary you don't need to be concerned about spelling or grammar. In any case, writing can play a significant role in developing creative communication skills.

In your diary world you can write using any language you wish, and you are allowed to misspell and create words of your own.

You make the rules! The emphasis in diary writing is to connect with the emotional, spontaneous and intuitive part of your Self.

Here are some guidelines for writing more colorful pieces. Even if the reader of your diary is just yourself, it never hurts to make the writing as interesting as possible to read.

How to write interesting reading

Gather a selection of your writing, choosing the oldest piece of text you have written. Ask yourself the following questions, and then revise the text based on your answers.

1. **What is the most important idea in the text, or what is the *focus* of the text?**

Circle or underline a word or the sentence expressing the most important idea.

2. **What actually *happened* to or in you?**

How have you described this event? Have you described it accurately? Underline the text where you do this.

3. **How did you *feel* when you wrote the piece of text?**

Are your feelings expressed in the writing? Do they come through clearly? Add words describing your emotions.

4. **What *details* have you described?**

Describe the details rather than generalizations. Circle or underline the details. Add descriptions of what you can *hear, see, smell, feel or touch.*

5. **Did you *show,* describe and demonstrate, rather than tell?**

If you say "The scenery was indescribable," you as a reader are going to become bored very quickly. A reader needs to know why something moved you, why you had the reaction you describe, or what made your heart beat so fast — not just that it happened.

6. **Does your *ending* connect with the *beginning*?**

Read the first two sentences of the piece, then the ending. Is there a connection at the end with the idea or images described in the first sentences? You're completing a circle with the ending, making the text complete by referring to the beginning.

7. **What did you *learn* from this experience you are writing about?**

Write about it at the end as if you were a reporter, assessing the event or emotions.

8. **Did the experience make you *wish* for something?**

Write about this too.

9. **What would you *name* your text?**

Give it a title.

Now, *rewrite* the text paying attention to your answers to these questions.

WRITING ABOUT YOUR IDEAL LIFE

B eginning a diary about how you imagine your ideal life is a powerful starting place to put *The Write Life Diary* concept into practice. Most of us have wishes and dreams about what we'd like to accomplish in our lives, how we envision ourselves in relationships, what kind of meaningful work we'd like to pursue. If your life is or isn't where you'd like it to be, writing daily to examine and define what you want as an alternative is enlightening and energizing, a catalyst for change.

To write a daily diary about creating your ideal life, here are seven tips for writing to explore and develop the possibilities you imagine — or want to imagine.

1. Choose a specific area of your life you would like to match your ideals, and write about it. This could be your career, love life, family etc.

2. Write in whatever form you find most comfortable: a poem, a list, a description, a short story.

3. Draw a picture or paste in a photo if you wish.

4. Use metaphors if you find this makes writing easier.

5. Give yourself one rule: write as if your ideal future exists already, in the present! Write in the present tense (happens / is now), use active verbs (not conditional or "ifs"). For example, "Fluent and funny, witty and wise, I'm standing tall and confident on the stage in front of an appreciative crowd of more than 500 hundred fully enraptured and appreciative listeners who encourage me further to tell my story."

6. After rereading your entry, give it a title or a heading.

7. Date the page.

The Wheel of Life is a useful tool to identify the various areas of your life that you want to bring to balance. These eight sections in the Wheel of Life represent different aspects of your life. You can choose different ones than what is included here, this is just an example. Here is how you use it: think of the center of the wheel as 0 and the outer edge as 10, rank your level of satisfaction from dissatisfaction (0) to very satisfied (10) with each life area by drawing a line to create a new outer edge. The new perimeter represents the wheel of your life. Looking at this graph of your life, ask yourself: if this were a real wheel, how bumpy would the ride be?

Your opportunity is to work with the the aspects of your life that your were dissatisfied with. You can use *The Write Life Diary* to describe the ideal reality by writing details how you are fulfilled and satisfied in these area.

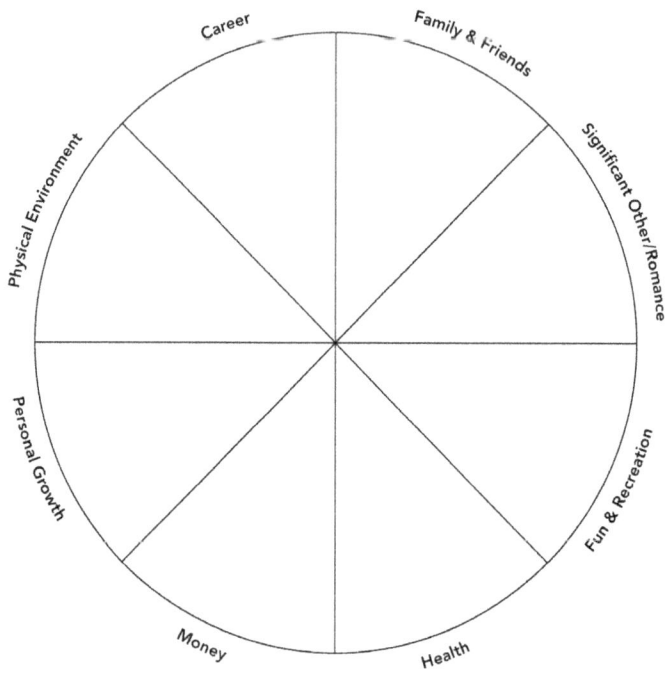

THE DUAL-COLUMN WRITING TECHNIQUE

Almost 40 years ago, Synectics® Corporation, a world leader in creative problem-solving, introduced an effective writing technique called "In-Out Listening." This special dual-column note-taking technique helps you to tap into your creative capacity effectively in problem-solving situations. The technique is based on the fact that during the listening process — when you are listening to your associates, your boss, a lecturer, or a teacher — you naturally "drop out" or lose your concentration every few minutes.

During these day-dreaming moments, there is a creative overflow of associations, vivid imagery, ideas, and other images passing through the mind. If you quickly make a note of them on one half of your notebook page, you can later study their meaning. The other side of the page can be used in the standard fashion, for writing the familiar, factual meeting or lecture notes.

Integrating the Synectics® principles into *The Write Life Diary* technique, gives you an opportunity to use the Future column for the doodling or writing from your unconscious while writing primary notes about your current situation on the Today column. This allows you to write two stories at the same time! You can be recording your daily events, feelings and thoughts on the right side of the page, in a column which labeled Today, leaving the left side for more creative material about your ideal life on the left labeled Future.

This is what I suggest you do:

Start with the Today column as a warm-up. Write about anything you choose, and in any way you please. Jump into the Future column every now and then when a thought pops in your head. In the Future column, allow yourself to dream, wish and role-play. Write about the best imaginable life you can create for yourself as if you had it all already! When you write in the left column, forget all the limitations on your everyday reality. In this column, you can write and create anything you want. Finally, date your description of the ideal future, either a month or a year ahead.

As the left column describes your vision for a better, more fulfilling future, it also becomes a powerful tool for you. These decisively positive affirmations that you have created for yourself and written down begin filling more space in your mind, and thus guide you to make choices directing you towards your ideal life. In these two columns, not only have you recorded a fascinating autobiography, both present and future life, but you have claimed full responsibility for your life — for right now and in the future. The following is an illustration of how I did it a long time ago.

FUTURE: 1/30/1995	**TODAY:** 1/ 30/ 1994
I'm rolling on the floor of the living room playing with my cuddly apricot toy poodle puppy Candy Kisses. *She is sweet natured and lifts my spirits just being around. When I write she curls up in my lap and sleeps contently – it just makes my heart sing!*	*What a day! I forgot my key in the house and had to call Olli to come from work to let me in. It was so annoying and I'm really angry at myself for being so sloppy. He was annoyed too but gracious enough to come and let me in in the middle of his busy day.* *I'm pretty certain that we will at some point get a dog. I really miss having a dog in the house. I fondly remember the dogs of my childhood: Manolito and Nappi and all neighbors' dogs... I miss that companionship and fun.*

Doodling your story

Sometimes it is hard to get started. Mindmapping (developed by Tony Buzan) and clustering (developed by Gabrielle Rico) are writing techniques that are designed to release more of your creative potential. These techniques break the linearity of conventional writing and tap into the imagination, emotions, and images of the writer.

The techniques have evolved from research, which has shown that our brain's left and right hemispheres operate differently.

Using mindmapping or clustering allows the pattern-seeking right side of your brain to win over the critical censor of the left hemisphere. This in turn "relieves the familiar anxiety about what to say and where to start and opens us to the freedom of expression we knew in childhood," says Rico. Together they empower your creativity. Here is how you can explore this technique.

1. In the upper third of a blank sheet of paper, write "My Future" and draw a circle around it.

2. Write words— uninhibited, uncensored — everything and anything that comes to your mind around this theme. After writing a word, draw a circle around it.

3. When you have finished, look how the words are connected to the central theme, My Future, and to each other.

Now to the fun part: writing about your Future – as if it was happening now. When you are describing your Future you need to step into it as if you were experiencing it and going through it or as if it had just happened already.

In the Synectics© process note-taking is done in two columns on a page: the right column is reserved for the factual notes from a presentation or lecture or meeting memo. The left side, on the other hand is for notes of your own creative connections, ideas and associations. Modeling after the brilliant Synectics© method, you will be using the left column for more creative writing and the right column for more factual documenting of what is going on in your life.

FUTURE: {add a date for a week, a month or a year from today}	TODAY: {add today's date}
1. Describe the SOLUTIONS and JOYS of your future Anything is possible! 2. Write ONLY POSITIVE STATEMENTS. Disregard all negative words (not, no, never) and negative expressions (don't, didn't, wasn't). Write this entry as the opposite to the problems you describe in the Today column. 3. Use the ACTIVE voice (write as if the event was happening now; also imply *who* does *what* (e.g. "I deal with the office manager directly about the matter"). Avoid passive sentences (e.g."The matter was dealt with"). 4. Write only in the PRESENT TENSE as if you were going through the experience right now (ex. "I'm ecstatic about the result"). Avoid conditional (e.g. If I were...it would be...).	1. Write this section first as a warm-up. Write about a challenge or an event any way you want. For instance: 2. What you have accomplished? What results did you get? What have you discussed with someone recently? How do you feel? Describe how your interaction progessed. What was her or his response? Were there misunderstanding or disappointments? 3. Write your thoughts about yourself, your family and relationships, work, life in general. 4. Describe events and activities during the day, previous events, dreams, people you have met, what you have learned. 5. Write a commentary about the news, movies, events, weather and how they affect your mood.

5. Include YOURSELF in the description.

6. Speak of changes happening in YOU.

7. Be as SPECIFIC as you can.

8. Remember that YOU are your only audience. Have the courage to dream BIG and write about it!

6. Lists the personal issues you need to deal with.

7. Describe your today's problems and challenges. E.g.
"I am anxious to ..."
"I feel devastated by ..."
"I hate to see ..."

8. Describe the joys you are encountering today
"I love ..."
"I'm so happy for ..."
"I was delighted that ..."

You can copy and use this sample page for your own diary writing.

Future: _____ ____ / ____ 20____	√	Today: _____ ____ / ____ 20____

THE POWER BOX

I t is important to write your diary in a language that is personally empowering, rather than using one that drags down your self-esteem. To identify important words in this positive, energizing language, you will need to identify them for yourself and write them in a Power Box. The Power Box is a box drawn at the bottom of the diary page. Once you have finished writing your description about your ideal future, select a few words from the text that — at the time of writing – feel most important to you based on the emotions they trigger. Then write these words into the Power Box at the bottom of the page. These emotionally loaded words will serve as simple affirmations and touchstones for future diary entries.

Future: _____ _____ / _____ 20_____	√	Today: _____ _____ / _____ 20_____
The Power Box for the affirmative words Cuddly, apricot toy poodle, play		

The power words you select identify the essence of your future. When you later browse through your diary, a glance at these words will trigger familiar, positive emotions in you. For example, my perennial power words include "energy," "healthy," "radiant," "happy," "wealth," "relaxed," "love," "friendship," and "laughter." Words can have different significance for different people; a friend has a great attachment to the word "power." While some power words change as you change, others can remain with you for longer periods of time.

CHECKING OFF SUCCESS

As you get used to writing about your future it is fun to go back to reading about your dreams, goals and hopes to acknowledge when they have become reality. To track the progress of events and goals as they happen in your life after you have dreamt and written about them, add a third column between the two main columns. This column is for marking off the "dreams come true" diary entries. The checking off exercise once a year adds excitement and fun to your writing.

Since this diary is meant to be a positive power tool, I do not recommend checking off anything that did not take place or that turned out negatively. When this happens, I trust that I might need to wait a little bit longer. Sometimes, things we regard as mistakes or disappointments in our lives can turn out to be opportunites for something new that we are were not able to imagine. Often it is only later when the wisdom reveals itself. However, if we dwell on disappointments and immerse ourselves in self-pity because we are too impatient for an outcome, we may miss the meaning. Impatience, in turn, may lead to misinterpretation.

If something you really wanted turns out not to be happening, and this is making you unhappy, just wait a little longer. Wait another week or a month, or perhaps a year. I prefer to wait at least two months before checking something off because it allows me to look at the bigger picture, and to perhaps adjust to a new situation. When you have written your affirmations, release them as if you were sending them off on a trip, not knowing when or if they will return with an answer.

Periodically check how accurate your visions were by rereading the positive visions you have created and described in yur diary can turn them into powerful affirmations. However, do not erase or mark the result as "failed" if something else has happened. Sometimes good things take longer to manifest themselves than we expect, and sometimes better things happen than we imagined. Mark the date when you checked off the event. You may want to make other check ups later.

An example from my old diary:

Future: 3/30/1995	√	Today: 1/25/1995
Thanks to the favorable currency exchange rates we are profiting extra when we sell our condo. We start to search for a house in earnest, and we find our dream house quickly. "This is it," we exclaim when we walk in our new home for the first time. It is spacious but cozy, welcoming yet provides privacy. It is a haven for our souls. It has a personality that matches well with our values. My office is a happy place to work in: light, bright, and it is separated from the rest of the house. I make friends easily with the neighbors.	√ 4/25/95 Closing	Finally, there's interest in our condo. This couple from Lohja have raised their offer but are still unsure and cannot finalize the deal yet. Shoot! Happily, there is another couple interested. The wife had fallen for the place and is now trying to convince her husband... We can do nothing but wait

Your Write Life Diary pages:

Future: _____ ____ / ____ 20____	√	Today: _____ ____ / ____ 20____

TIME TRAVEL WITH YOUR DIARY

Diary writing provides a fantastic opportunity to do whatever you want with your life. One of the most fascinating things is time travel. Just as writing a diary about what happened to you today and in the future you can go down the memory lane and write about past events and insights — almost in a memoir style. Time travel expands your understanding of yourself. I'm suggesting that you can be even bolder with your past and create a story about your history, one that is made up of whatever you want. Sometimes it is healing to go back in time and rewrite the story you have gotten used to telling yourself about your life. In the same way that you write in your diary about hopes and dreams for the future, you can dream up that you are living your dearest wishes and hopes in the past, creating the most happy childhood — even if you didn't have one. Yes, this sounds a bit like a fiction writing exercise. But how about it? It will certainly get your creative juices going.

So far, I've shown you how to use diary writing to outline your present day experiences and how you can write about the future as if it was already true. Now try your hand rewriting your past to describe what you want it to be.

In your diary, follow the roads not taken, explore the *what ifs*, get rid of the burdening and bitter baggage from the pains of the past and begin to live in the beauty of this moment.

Instructions for rewriting the Past

Here are the instructions for your rewriting exercise. Write about a past event in the right hand column, being as specific as you can remember, outlining all the pain you felt. In the left, doodling column rewrite the story as if you were living it with a resolution more to your liking.

REWRITE THE PAST: {add the date from the past experience you want to rewrite}	THE PAST MEMORY: {add today's date}
Write here with a follow-up to the story in the right column. Rewrite a painful memory or a traumatic experience from your childhood. • "Become" the person you were when the unhappy event took place. Be that person again in the present tense, writing how things happened in the now. • Now pretend that nothing	Write this part first as a warm-up. Write anything you remember as specifically as you can about a past event that brought you grief. For example, write about your most painful memory or a major traumatic event in your childhood. • Meditate briefly. • Doodle key words about

bad ever happened. How is it different now when things go well?

- Change this dramatic experience into a description of something else that would have made you happy.

- Write the opposite scenario for what you originally experienced by treating the event as if it turned out in a positive way.

- Turn everything upside down and make this event the happiest moment of your life.

- Be bold and lie about it!

- It is your life and you can write a fictional story about what happened if you so wish!

- Describe the SOLUTIONS and JOYS of the past event.

- Write ONLY in the POSITIVE VOICE — disregard all negative words (not, no, never) and include negative

all kinds of childhood memories on a fresh page of paper.

- Select one.

- Dwell in that memory.

- Start writing.

For instance:

Write about:
⇒ Describe what *really* happened during the event you are describing: when and where it took place, who was involved, what happened, how were you affected, you felt then, how you feel about things now, and how this event is connected to your current reality.

⇒ Your memories and disappointments.

Describe, for example:
⇒ Problems and challenges
"I was anxious/disappointed to ..."
"I felt devastated by ..."
"I hated to see ..."

expressions (don't, didn't, wasn't). Write the opposite to the problems or difficulties you experienced in the past.

- Use the ACTIVE voice (as if the event was happening now; also imply who does what (e.g. "I deal with the office manager directly about the matter.")

- Avoid passive sentences. and passive verbs. (ex. "The matter was dealt with").

- Write only in the PRESENT TENSE as if you were going through the experience right now (e.g.. "I'm ecstatic about the result"). Avoid conditional words. (e.g. If I were…it would be…)

- Include YOURSELF.

- Speak of a change in YOU.

- Be as SPECIFIC as you can. Describe the details through all your senses: what you see, hear, feel, touch, smell.

• Remember that YOU are your only audience. Be bold in your writing and write a big happy lie — it's your life! You can do whatever you like with it! • Write what you are now learning from this experience.

Now, instead of gathering the most affirming words for the Power Box, use it to write our key *learnings* from this experience. Make a tick mark beside an issue when you feel you have dealt with it and you can put it behind you. Do this when you are ready to move on.

Future: _____ _____ / _____ 20_____	√	Today: _____ _____ / _____ 20_____

The Power Box for "the learnings" words

PRACTICING THE WRITE LIFE DIARY

Developing any skill requires practice. The same principle applies to *The Write Life Diary.* Writing to create positive changes and fulfillment in your life requires starting with small steps, with small actions. It is the repetition that sets the stage and builds the receptivity allowing things to happen. It is not a new concept. According to Aristotle: *"We are what we repeatedly do. Excellence, then, is not an act, but a habit."* It is the routine that counts. Although my hope is to write in my diary regularly, daily if I can, I will never force myself do it. Forcing creates resentment and there is no need for this! For example, someone once asked whether I feared something uncontrollably terrible would happen to me if I neglected my writing. I replied saying, "There is never an outside mystical power that takes over when I write; it is my voice and it is for myself that I write. This is not witchcraft, it's willcraft."

I write whenever it suits me. However, I do remind myself of all the benefits of writing a daily diary entry, and recall how much I enjoy writing. I know my diary is always there when I need it.

I write when I seek a way to retreat to my secret haven, or when I'm searchng for clarity or sorting out my challenges or determine my priorities.

I also agree with Joyce Chapman who says, *"The act of writing makes thoughts become real and brings a deeper level of release than just verbal communication or thinking can do alone."* In another statement, she writes: *"In becoming a more confident writer, I was becoming a confident creator of my life. I began to ask myself questions and discover my own answers."*

Trust your intuition and let your life unfold organically onto the pages of your diary. Soon you will discover you are not only developing the story of your life but you are developing yourself and enjoying the process.

Here is a summary of key concepts in *The Write Life Diary*:

- In your personal diary you can write anything – even lie!
- Keep it positive
- Write in the present tense
- Split each page into two columns: one for the current reality, one for the ideal

EPILOGUE – writing the living, living the writing

Bertrand Russell said, *"What then can a man do who is unhappy because he is encased in self? So long as he continues to think about the causes of his unhappiness, he continues to be self-centered and therefore does not get outside the vicious circle." "[A happy] man feels himself a citizen of the universe, enjoying freely the spectacle that it offers and the joys that it affords, untroubled by the thought of death because he feels himself not really separate from those who will come after him. It is in such profound instinctive union with the stream of life that the greatest joy is to be found."*

I trust you will enjoy writing and creating the exciting story of your very own life using the tools of *The Write Life Diary.* I wish you fulfillment and joy as you practice your diary writing. Enjoy the move from frustration to purpose and direction. Enjoy the process of learning to trust your intuition and ability to create. The future you create through the pages of your diary will be an expression of everything you treasure and believe essential to a rich life; you will find it becomes a map of your values. This, in turn, will allow you to get closer to the ultimate purpose of our human experience: Know Thyself.

And, please, keep me posted!
Kristiina

ABOUT THE AUTHOR

KRISTIINA HIUKKA writes and teaches her *The Write Life Diary* concept for individual students and groups. A native of Finland, she now resides in the Pacific Northwest. She is also a sought-after speaker and professional coach, leading workshops that energize and inspire leaders and their teams into alignment and action.

For more information about Kristiina's availablity as a speaker or as an instructor, or to discuss questions about *The Write Life Diary,* please contact her at
kristiina@thewritelifediary.com.

APPENDICES

APPENDIX 1: How to make diary writing interesting and fun

1. Write at least the date on top of the page every day. Remember, empty pages communicate too.

2. Write about flowers —and let them become descriptions of people in your life or special moments.

3. Use different colored pens for various days.

4. Write about the best thing in your day.

5. Write about the worst thing in your day.

6. Describe a specific moment.

7. Write *to-do* lists.

8. Compose *people-that-I-need-to-meet* or *would like to-meet* lists.

9. Write no longer than 10 or 15 minutes, timing yourself with a kitchen timer or an alarm clock.

10. Keep a weekly, monthly or yearly diary, and write entries on the same day of the same week, month or year.

11. Write regularly: in the evening, morning, during a lunch break.

12. Jot down a single adjective, choosing one word to describe your day, your feelings or experiences just for that day.

13. Pick a theme for a day or week or a month, and describe everything through that theme; examples: clarity, anger, passion, change, love, friendship...

14. Write poetry, a short story or something descriptive.

15. Write a dialogue (with other people, events, animals or yourself).

16. Describe a stranger as if you knew that person well.

17. Describe a person you think you know with as much detail as you can.

18. Jot down something you learned today, or write something about your beliefs and philosphy, or about a deep or religious revelation.

19. Ponder about the meaning of a quotation or something you heard or some graffiti you saw.

20. Write ten things you want to accomplish tomorrow, this week, this month or this year.

21. Write about your dreams or fantasies.

22. Write a letter to yourself. Console yourself, encourage yourself, be a friend to yourself.

23. Doodle a cartoon or draw a picture.

24. Write a prayer.

25. Write without thinking, stream of consciousness entry. Then read it, and think and write about its meaning to you. Did it reveal something unexpected?

26. Write jokes, fairy tales or stories.

27. Write the biggest lie of your life, even if you make it up.

28. Start your entry with a question (e.g. Why am I getting irritated by X?).

29. Make a statement or express an opinion (e.g. X makes me mad).

30. Keep what you write short and simple (KISS).

31. Write through your senses: express how you feel, what you see, what you hear.

32. Write about yourself as you think others see you; write with a particular person's eyes or from a view point.

33. Sketch a character in your life, work place or home).

34. Pick an object or an animal and write about its life, how it feels and sees the world, and what it thinks of you (e.g. the refrigerator in your house, your favorite armchair, your car, your dog, your fish).

35. Collect a set of sentences to begin an entry (e.g. I'm proud of myself because... My biggest fear/wish/secret... Today I accomplished / achieved / met...). Select a different beginning each day.

36. Begin writing with a brief meditation.

37. Write while istening to relaxing background music.

38. Draw a circle or a box and fill it with words that spontaneously enter your mind.

39. Describe major events in you life: birth, school, children, marriage, divorce, jobs, or any important date in your life.

40. Write about your reaction to a world event.

41. Write about money: what you wish to do with it, how you feel about it, how you earn it and spend it.

42. Write about a grief or sorrow.

43. Write about your goals and wishes.

44. Write about love and sex, your enthusiasms or lack of it.

45. Write about something you can see, hear, smell, taste or touch.

46. Paste a photo or an image in your diary, give it a title, describe its meaning to you, or just leave it as it is. Remember to date the page.

47. Keep a journal about your dreams.

48. Keep a travel journal.

49. Keep a weather journal.

50. Keep a garden journal.

51. Keep a birthday journal (e.g. what you do or give for the birthdays of your family members and friends).

52. Keep a dinner journal (e.g. write the recipes of your favorite meals each week and who participated in the dinner).

53. Keep a journal about cultural events (e.g. movies, theater outings or concerts).

54. Organize your letters into a folder to make a journal of your correspondence. Also include copies of your own letters to other people.

55. Write about your political reflections.

56. Write a peculiar or strange word in the middle of the paper, write how and why you came to think about that word.

57. Respect the blank page: date it and go on.

58. Don't worry about spelling or grammar when you set out to write. Be your own editor later, when you read your text in a month or two!

59. Name to your diary and approach writing in it as if talking to a friend.

60. Break your experiences into categories and tackle just one at a time: work, love, family, house, friendship.

61. Keep a list of inspiring words handy, for example: anger, love, senses, emotions, learning, challenge, surprise, smile...

62. Stir up your emotions, then describe what and how you feel.

63. Sharpen your hearing, then describe what you hear.

64. Be clear and focused; describe what you see.

65. Describe your location and how it makes you feel.

66. Describe what you have been doing all day.

67. Describe the person(s) who you have been with that day.

68. Describe of the groups you are part of and how you fit in .

69. Challenge your intelligence and debate an issue with yourself. Draw conclusions and describe the consequences.

70. Trust your intuition.

71. Let go of trying to have your writing be perfect.

72. Go outdoors for a walk and take a note pad with you.

73.   Take a nap. Write in your diary as soon as you wake up.

74.   Decide what is your personal best time of the day to write.

75.   Write when you are emotional. Read whast you've written when you are calm.

76.   Pay attention to ergonomics and write in a comfortable position.

77.   Write in good light.

78.   First read a passage from a book, then write anything that comes to mind.

79.   Draw graphic models before you write.

80.   Be a copycat: try to adapt somebody else's style of writing for example, Ernest Hemingway.

81.   Apply a project plan to your writing; for example, before you start, decide how much you want to write every day or once a week, and what you want to accomplish. Write it down.

82.   Think and write about how you might help other people.

83.   Keep different journals for different moods.

84.   Write a newsletter about your life to your friends and relatives.

85.   Imagine what your dog would write about you.

86.   End with: what did I learn today? Or what did I learn from this experience?

87.   Give your text a title. Choose a key word or a theme.

88.   Tie the final sentence back to the beginning idea of your daily entry.

89.   Think of your writing as only a draft.

90.   Imagine you are writing a newspaper editorial about the most important issue in your life.

91.   Imagine yourself writing a column in your local newspaper or your favorite magazine.

92.   Learn about creative writing techniques from other books or workshops.

93.   Show with your writing, do not tell!

94.   Explore process writing; for example, begin with a word or an outline, fill in the main details the second time round, and finally, write out the complete story.

95.   Keep notebooks around the house to pick up and write in whenever you are near.

96.   Keep a journal about your hopes, goals and affirmations.

97.   Keep a diary on your computer.

98.   Write with your non-dominant hand.

99.   Choose a newspaper headline and write your story below it.

100.   Believe that anything is possible- write about your most audacious dreams.

101.   Know thyself: write anything you know about yourself.

102.   Be patient. The words will come.

103.   Read other diary entries, your own from the past or something new.

104.   Read, read, read! For ideas and inspiration.

105. Make word strings; e.g. choose a word and let it inspire another, then let that one inspire a third word, and so on.

106. Keep lists of your favorite words or phrases for inspiration.

APPENDIX 2: Time travel writing

THE PAST	THE PRESENT	THE FUTURE
Writing exercise: Write 15 minutes about a major traumatic event in your childhood, the worst painful memory you recall years later.	Writing exercise: Write 15 minutes about the most important thing that happened to you today.	Writing exercise: Write 15 minutes about your wishes and goals for your future.
Doodle ideas. Select one. Start writing.		Make a list of areas of your life (ex. relationships, work, school, etc.) Choose one.
		Doodle ideas about what you want to include in your writing . Write about your goals.
Typically, we write about the past in the past tense. *I was, I did this, I saw that*	Typically, we write about the present in the present or past tense. *I am, I do this, I saw that*	Typically we write about the future in the future tense or conditional. *I will be / I would be / I wish I was…*

Writing exercise: Rewrite the event you described before in the present tense and make it as positive an occasion as possible. If it were something painful that you described, pretend and change the event into being something good.

Writing exercise: Rewrite the event as it happened now, putting it in the present tense

Writing exercise: Rewrite your hopes and goals by eliminating all "I wish" and "I hope" sentences. Rewrite your hopes and goals again in the present tense, as if they were your reality now.

APPENDIX 3: The Write Life Diary sample page

Future: _____ ____ / ____ 20____	√	Today: _____ ____ / ____ 20____

RELATED READING

A Course in Miracles, Text, Workbook for students, Manual for teachers, 1992. Glen Ellen: Foundation for Inner Peace.

Averill, James & Elma Nunley, Voyages of the heart, Living an emotionally creative life, 1992. Free Press

Barry Beyerstein & Dale Beyerstein, editors. The Write stuff--evaluations of graphology, 1992. Buffalo: Prometheus Books.

Biffle, Christopher, A journey through your childhood: A write-in guide for reliving your past, clarifying your present and charting your future, Inner Work Book.

Boldt, Laurence, Zen and the art of making a living. A practical guide to creative career design, 1993. Penguin Arkana.

Bolles, Richard Nelson, What color is your parachute? 1994. Ten Speed Press.

Canfield, Jack & Mark Victor **Hansen**, The Aladdin Factor, 1995. New York: Berkeley.

Cameron, Julia, The Artist's Way. A spiritual path to higher creativity, 1992. New York: G.P. Putnam's Sons.

Capacchione, Lucia, Ph D, The creative journal: The art of finding yourself, 1979. North Hollywood: Newcastle Publishing.

Capacchione, Lucia, Ph D, The creative journal for children, A guide for parents, teachers and counselors, 1989. Boston & London: Sambhala.

Capacchione, Lucia, Ph D, The creative journal for teens. Making friends with yourself, 1992. North Hollywood: Newcastle Publishing.

Carson, Gayle, Winning ways, 1988. Miami: G. Carson.

Chaney, Marti & Vicki **Thayer**, Imagine loving your work, 1989. Berkeley: Celestial Arts.

Chapman, Joyce, Journaling for joy: Writing your way to personal growth and freedom, 1991. North Hollywood: Newcastle Publishing.

Edwards, Gill, Living magically, 1991. London: Judy Piatkus.

Edwards, Gill, Stepping into the magic, 1993. London: Judy Piatkus.

Emery, Marcia, Intuition workbook, 1995. Englewood Cliffs: Prentice Hall.

Gawain, Shakti, Creative visualization, 1995 (revised edition). San Raphael: New World Library.

Gershon, David & Gail **Straub**, Empowerment: The art of creating your life as you want it, 1989. New York: Dell Publishing.

Hay, Louise, You can heal your life, 1987. Carson: Hay House.

Hoff, Benjamin, The Tao of Pooh, 1982. Penguin books.

Holmes, Marjorie, Writing articles from the heart: How to write and sell your life experiences, 1993. Writers digest books.

Jeffers, Susan, *Feel the fear and do it anyway*, 1987. London: Arrow Books.

Keen, Sam & Anne Valley-Fox, Your mythic journey: Finding meaning in your life through writing and storytelling, Inner Work Book.

Mackay, Harvey, Sharkproof, 1993. London: Piatkus.

Morgan, Marlo, Mutant message from down under, 1994.

Morrisey, George, Creating your future. Personal strategic planning for professionals, 1992. San Francisco: Barrett-Koehler Publications.

Peale, Norman Vincent, The power of positive thinking.

Peck, M. Scott, A world to be born, 1993. London: Rider.

Progoff, Ira, At journal workshop: Writing to access power of the unconscious and evoke creative ability, 1975, 1992. New York:Putnam.

Rainer, Tristine, The new diary, 1978. New York: Jeremy P. Tarcher/Perigee Books.

Rico, Gabriele, Writing the natural way, 1983. New York: A. Jeremy P. Tarcher/Putnam.

Rico, Gabriele, Pain and possibility: Writing your way through personal crisis. Inner Work Book.

Robbins, Anthony, Giant steps, 1994. New York: Fireside.

Robbins, Anthony, Unlimited power, 1988. London: Simon Schuster.

Roman, Sanaya, Personal power, 1986. Tiburon: HJ Kramer.

Russell, Bertrand, The conquest of happiness, 1958. New York: Liveright.

Seidman, Michael, Living the dream. An outline for a life in fiction, 1992. Carroll & Graf.

Senge, Peter, The fifth discipline, 1990. New York: Doubleday.

Shone, Ronald, Creative visualization: How to use imagery and imagination for self improvement, 1980. Rochester: Destiny Books.

Sinetar, Marsha, To build the life you want, create the work you love, 1995. St Martin's Press.

Sinetar, Marsha, Do what you love and money will follow, 1987. New York: Paulist Press.

Tice, Lou, A better world, a better you, 1989. Englewood Cliffs: Prentice Hall.

Trafford, Angela Passidomo, The heroic path, 1993. Carson: Hay House.

Whelen, Dolores, Your breaking point, 1993. Dublin: Attic Press.

Writing My Life from Good to Great
Journal by

_____

The Write Life Diary™ method

Instructions for writing The Write Life Diary™

TODAY {add today's date}
Write first as a warm-up. Ideas to write about: your dreams, celebrations, challenges, thoughts and feelings about yourself, your family and relationships, work, events, activities, people you have met, what you have learned, accomplished or discussed with someone recently; commentary about the news, movies, weather and how they affect your mood.

FUTURE {add a date a week, a month or a year from today}
Describe as specifically as you can how you solve problems and revel in the joyful flow of your life using positive statements. Disregard negative words (not, no, never) and negative expressions (don't, didn't, wasn't). Use the active voice and the present tense as if you were going through the experience right now. Avoid conditional and passive sentences. Include yourself in the description. Since you are your only audience, you can audaciously write about your boldest dreams.

POWER BOX
Select a few emotionally powerful words from your journaling on the Future page that feel most intriguing to you. Write these words into the Power Box at the bottom of the page. These emotionally loaded "power" words will serve as simple affirmations and touchstones.

CHECK OFF
In this column mark off the "dreams come true" diary entries on the Future page. The periodic checking off exercise adds excitement to your writing.

Future: _____ _____ /_____20_____

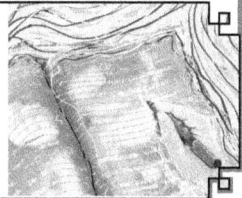

Future: _____ _____ / _____ 20_____

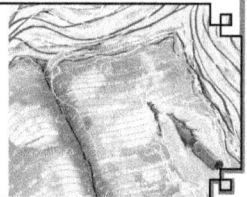

Future: _____ _____ / _____20_____

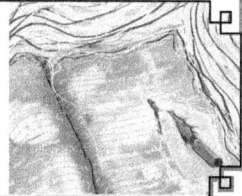

Future: _____ _____ /_____ 20_____

Today: _____ _____ / _____ 20 _____

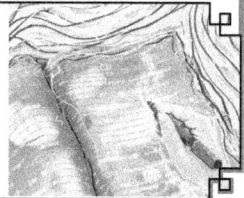

Future: _____ _____ / _____ 20 _____

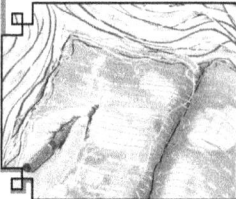

Today: _____ ____ / ____ 20____

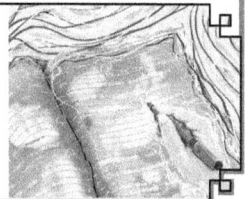

Future: _____ _____ / _____20_____

Today: _____ _____ / _____ 20 _____

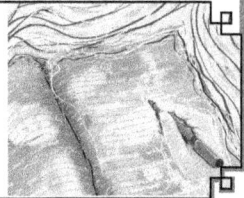

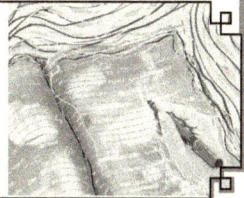

Future: _____ _____ /_____ 20_____

Today: _____ _____ /_____20_____

Future: _____ _____ / _____ 20 _____

Today: _____ ____ / ____ 20____

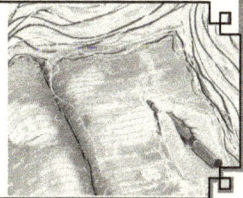

Future: _____ _____ /_____ 20_____

Today: _____ _____ / _____ 20_____

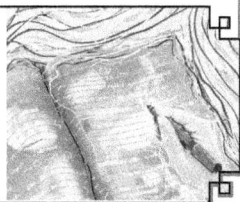

Future: _____ _____ / _____20_____

Today: _____ _____ /_____20_____

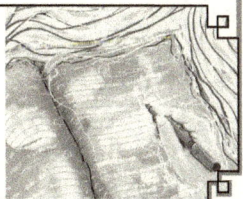

Today: _____ _____ /_____20_____

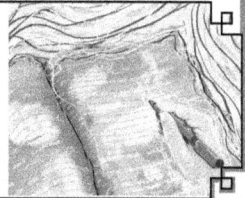

Today: _____ _____ / _____ 20_____

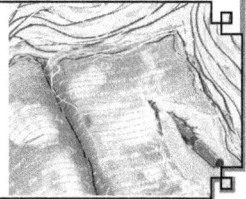

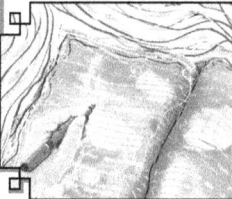

Today: _____ _____ /_____20_____

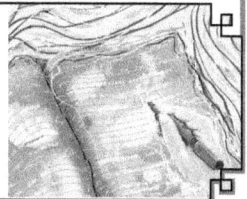

Future: _____ _____ / _____20_____

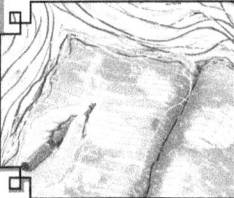

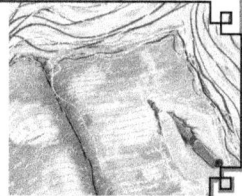

Today: _____ _____ / _____ 20_____

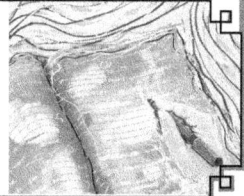

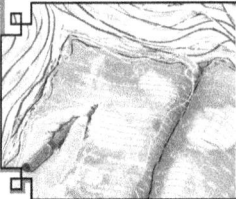

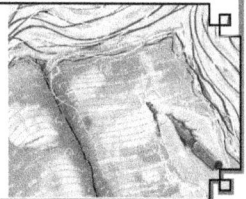

Future: _____ ____ /____20____

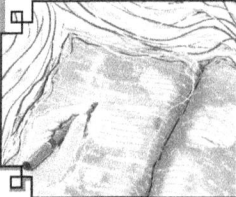

Today: _____ _____ / _____ 20_____

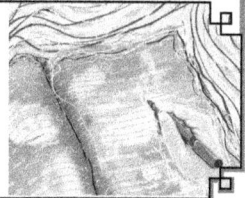

Future: _____ _____ /_____ 20_____

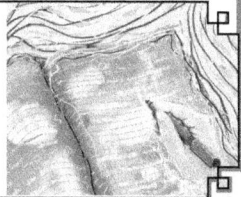

Future: _____ ____ /____20____

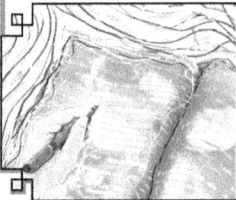

Today: _____ _____ /_____20_____

www.ingramcontent.com/pod-product-compliance
Lightning Source LLC
Chambersburg PA
CBHW051815040426

42446CB00007B/675